W. B. YEATS

IMAGES OF IRELAND

W. B. YEATS

IMAGES OF IRELAND

ALAIN LE GARSMEUR · BERNARD McCABE

LITTLE, BROWN AND COMPANY

BOSTON · TORONTO · LONDON

For Anna Carragher and Jane McCabe

Photographs copyright © 1991 Alain Le Garsmeur
Introduction copyright © 1991 Bernard McCabe

First published in Great Britain in 1991 by
Little, Brown and Company (UK) Limited
Beacon House, 30 North End Road, London W14 0SH

The publishers wish to thank the following for permission
to reproduce the photographs in the Introduction:
Hulton-Deutsch Collection p.15; Irish Tourist Board p.16;
Mander and Mitchenson Theatre Collection pp.12, 18;
Mansell Collection pp.9,11.

ISBN 0-316-88861-3
A CIP catalogue record for this book
is available from the British Library

10 9 8 7 6 5 4 3 2 1

Designed by Bet Ayer
Typeset by DP Photosetting, Aylesbury, Bucks
Printed and bound in Italy by Arnoldo Mondadori

Opposite title page: Dunguaire Castle at Kinvara, Co. Clare.

CONTENTS

A BRIEF CHRONOLOGY   6

YEATS IN IRELAND   8

SLIGO   20

COOLE PARK   76

THOOR BALLYLEE   88

LAND OF HEART'S DESIRE   98

DUBLIN   140

INDEX   160

A BRIEF CHRONOLOGY

1865 William Butler Yeats born on 13 June in Sandymount, Dublin, to the portrait-painter John Butler Yeats and Susan Mary Yeats (née Pollexfen).

1867 The family moves to London. Yeats lives there for the next fourteen years, with many lengthy summer visits to his Pollexfen grandfather in Sligo.

1877–81 Yeats attends the Godolphin School in Hammersmith.

1881 The family returns to Dublin.

1881–84 Yeats attends the Erasmus Smith High School in Harcourt St, Dublin, where he meets Charles Johnston, a keen Theosophist.

1881–96 Spends most summers with his uncle, George Pollexfen, in Sligo.

1884 Enrols at Metropolitan School of Art, Kildare St, Dublin. Meets the poet George Russell (AE).

1885 Meets John O'Leary, the old Fenian and enthusiast of Irish literature. With Charles Johnston founds the Dublin Hermetic Society. Publishes first poems.

1886 Begins to make a precarious living as a man of letters; essays and reviews in various literary magazines in Ireland and England.

1887 Family moves to London again. Yeats joins London Theosophical Society. Lives in London for the next thirty-two years, makes frequent extended visits to Ireland.

1888 *Fairy and Folk Tales of the Irish Peasantry.*

1887–88 Moves into London's literary world; meets Oscar Wilde, William Morris, G.B. Shaw, W.E. Henley.

1889 *The Wanderings of Oisin and Other Poems.* Meets Maud Gonne, falls in love with her.

1890 Forms lifelong friendship with the actress Florence Farr,

Financial difficulties. Journalism in American newspapers, many reviews and essays in Dublin and London magazines. Founds the Rhymers' Club in London with the poet Lionel Johnson and others.

1891 *Representative Irish Tales* and *John Sherman*, his one novel. With O'Leary founds the Young Ireland League to promote Irish writing. First proposes marriage to Maud Gonne.

1892 *The Countess Kathleen; Irish Fairy Tales.* Founds in London the Irish Literary Society; in Dublin the National Literary Society.

1893 *The Celtic Twilight*, a collection of Sligo folk-tales. Edits *The Works of William Blake* and *The Poems of William Blake.*

1894 *The Land of Heart's Desire*, his first play to be produced. Meets Constance and Eva Gore-Booth at their mansion, Lissadell, in Sligo. Maud Gonne has a daughter, Iseult, by Lucien Millevoye.

1895 *Poems.* Begins his first love affair, with Olivia Shakespear.

1896 In Paris befriends the Irish playwright J.M. Synge; urges him to go to the Aran Islands. Joins Irish Republican Brotherhood.

1897 *The Secret Rose.* Spends the first of many summers at Lady Gregory's home, Coole Park, Co. Galway. They plan an Irish National Theatre.

1898 Makes the third of his many unsuccessful proposals to Maud Gonne.

1899 *The Wind among the Reeds* (poems). *The Countess Cathleen* produced in Dublin.

1900 His mother dies. Leaves Irish Republican Brotherhood.

1902 Becomes President of the Irish National Theatre Society. Yeats's father and sisters return to Dublin. *Cathleen ni Houlihan* produced in Dublin with Maud Gonne in title role.

1903 Publishes poems, *In the Seven Woods*; and essays, *Ideas of Good and*

Evil. Begins first American lecture tour. Maud Gonne marries Major John MacBride.

1904 Completes tour of America. Publishes play, *The King's Threshold*. Abbey Theatre opens and his *On Baile's Strand* is performed there on its first night. *Stories of Red Hanrahan*.

1905 A director of the Abbey Theatre.

1906 His *Deirdre* performed at the Abbey. *Poems 1899–1905*.

1907 Synge's *The Playboy of the Western World* at the Abbey greeted with riots. Yeats's father leaves Dublin permanently for New York. John O'Leary dies.

1908 *Collected Works* (eight volumes). Meets Ezra Pound in London.

1909 Synge dies of Hodgkin's disease. Yeats edits Synge's *Poems and Translations*.

1910 *The Green Helmet and Other Poems*. Receives Civil List pension of £150 a year. Resigns from the Abbey managership. His uncle Pollexfen dies.

1911 Meets Bertha Georgina Hyde-Lees.

1912 Protests when Dublin Corporation rejects Hugh Lane's gift of modern paintings to the city.

1913 Supports the workers in the Dublin Lock-out struggle. Shares lodgings in England with Pound; becomes interested in Japanese *Noh* plays.

1914 *Responsibilities: Poems and a Play*.

1915 Refuses knighthood.

1916 First autobiographical work, *Reveries over Childhood and Youth*. Continues his study of *Noh* drama. Begins his *Four Plays for Dancers*; the first, *At the Hawk's Well*, is performed in London. The Easter Rising in Dublin. Major John MacBride and several young literary friends among fifteen prisoners executed by the British. Again proposes marriage to Maud Gonne (now a widow); is refused. Proposes to Maud's daughter, Iseult; is refused.

1917 Buys a small ruined castle at Thoor Ballylee, Co. Galway, as summer home. Proposes to George Hyde-Lees; is accepted. Marries 20 October in London. Long sessions of automatic writing with his wife. *The Wild Swans at Coole* (poems).

1918 Lady Gregory's only son killed in the war. Yeats writes elegy for him. Essays, *Per Amica Silentia Lunae*.

1919 *The Only Jealousy of Emer* (play) published. His daughter, Anne Butler Yeats, born in Dublin. Yeats leaves London for good and moves to Oxford.

1920 Denounces British army atrocities in Ireland.

1921 His son, William Michael Yeats, born. Poems, *Michael Robartes and the Dancer*. In the Civil War Yeats supports Anglo-Irish Treaty.

1922 His father dies. More autobiography, *The Trembling of the Veil*. In December is made a senator of the new Irish Free State. Yeats now permanently established in Dublin.

1923 Awarded Nobel Prize for Literature.

1925 His mystical work, *A Vision*, based on dreams and automatic writing. Speaks in favour of divorce in the Irish Senate.

1926 His *Sophocles' King Oedipus* produced at the Abbey. Defends Sean O'Casey's *The Plough and the Stars* after riots at the Abbey.

1927 His *Sophocles' Oedipus at Colonus* produced there. Constance (Gore-Booth) Markievicz dies.

1928 Strongly attacks proposed censorship of books. *The Tower* (poems). In ill-health all year; leaves the Senate; winters in Rapallo.

1929 *Fighting the Waves* at the Abbey.

1930 *The Words upon the Window-Pane* at the Abbey.

1932 Helps establish Irish Academy of Letters. Lady Gregory dies. *Words for Music Perhaps, and Other Poems*.

1933 *The Winding Stair and Other Poems*. Briefly interested in General O'Duffy of the Blueshirts, a fascist group.

1934 Steinach vasectomy. Over next four years, a series of short affairs with younger women. *Collected Plays* and *The King of the Great Clock Tower*.

1935 Meets Lady Dorothy Wellesley, a minor poet. Begins literary correspondence with her. AE dies. *A Full Moon in March* (play). A third volume of autobiography, *Dramatis Personae*.

1936 Edits his controversial *The Oxford Book of Modern Verse*. Broadcasts on BBC on modern poetry.

1937 Much ill-health. Makes four broadcasts on the BBC of his own poetry. *Essays, 1931–6*.

1938 Goes to Menton, in south of France, for health's sake. First performances of *Purgatory*. *New Poems*. Works on his last play, *The Death of Cuchulain*.

1939 Dies in France, 28 January. Buried at Roquebrune. In 1948, in fulfilment of his wish, Yeats's remains are brought back to Ireland.

YEATS IN IRELAND

Ireland's mountains and lakes, its hills and valleys, its small towns and smaller villages are everywhere in Yeats's poetry. Places had an almost sacramental importance for him. Ben Bulben, Kiltartan, Corcomroe, the Seven Woods at Coole, the Tower at Ballylee – he was always a great chanter of name upon name:

> My cousin is priest in Kilvarnet,
> My brother in Mocharabuiee.

And as the names come and go in Yeats's verse, they breathe a pressing sense of the poet's deep affinities with them; these places belong to him, he belongs to them.

Yeats, in fact, lived much of his adult life in the city of Dublin. But the rural west of Ireland was crucial to him as a poet. His imagination ranged widely over Ireland – Tara and Cruachan, Cashel and Glendalough – but in the course of his creative life three places in Connaught came to dominate the poet's mind: Sligo in his twenties and thirties, in his late thirties and forties Coole Park in Galway, and in his fifties and sixties Thoor Ballylee in the same county. This book, therefore, begins by following Yeats through these western landscapes; it then takes a short excursion into other significant places in his rural Ireland, and, as he also led an intense and complex public and private life in Dublin, it ends with a series of images from that ancient city's present and past.

Yeats's imagination lived in non-Irish places, too, but these were rather landscapes of the mind: Renaissance palaces in Florence and Urbino, the golden smithies of Byzantium, the spiritualists's strange mansions. Our book does not follow the poet into those mysterious places, yet the extracts offered here *are* representative of his work. The constant oppositions of youth and age, of life and death, of hate and love, of body and spirit. We catch here the inimitable excitement, passion and drama of his verse, we hear its music and we savour the clarity and subtle intelligence of his prose.

Alain Le Garsmeur's photographs do not seek to re-create the Ireland that Yeats saw; instead they present what can still be seen now of what the poet looked at then. Yeats's work needs no visual enhancement, yet illustration has its own powerful and revealing virtues. The camera can put us in possession of

> Those images that yet
> Fresh images beget.

It can look afresh at Yeats's Ireland, both making it new and yet turning us back again to the extraordinary poetry that he made out of it.

SLIGO

In childhood and youth Sligo was everything to Yeats. Elsewhere he was an exile. He knew this already as a schoolboy, when, walking in the London streets, he 'longed for a sod of earth from some field that I knew, something of Sligo to hold in my hand'.

It is strange and beautiful country. If you walk out west from Sligo town past the harbour, you will soon come to Rosses Point, five miles from Sligo, 'a little sea-dividing sandy plain', and to 'Memory Harbour', once memorably painted by the poet's brother, Jack Yeats. Turning your back on the Atlantic and looking east you will see most of the hills and valleys that possessed Yeats's imagination from boyhood on. To the north lies the great mass of 'bare Ben

In 1905, at the age of forty, Yeats was made a director of the Abbey Theatre.

Beyond these familiarities loomed always the mysteries that emanated from Sligo's mountains and valleys and from the tales he was told about them. The local peasants knew the ancient but still living legends of love and war: Ben Bulben as the scene of a wild-boar hunt, at which Diarmuid was killed as he was eloping with Grainne; Knocknarea 'the cairn-heaped grassy hill/where passionate Maeve is stony-still . . .'. The place was full of magic, full of tales of danger and mystery that were part of daily life for the Sligo countrypeople. Mighty creatures were said to haunt nearby Inchy Wood, and at Rosses Point 'few countrymen would fall asleep under its low cliff, for he who sleeps here may wake ''silly'', the Sidhe having carried off his soul'.

The powerful and mysterious sense of place that Yeats absorbed from the Sligo landscape emerges most insistently in his early work, but it remained with him throughout his life. His play *At the Hawk's Well*, written when he was in his fifties, is set in the Ox Mountains near Coolaney, just south of Knocknarea, and in another play, *The King of the Great Clock Tower*, written in his seventieth year, all these place-names come flooding back: Castle Dargan, the Rosses, Ben Bulben, Knocknarea.

In Sligo the massive presence of those 'numinous hills' and the talk of the people who lived among them, fed his growing need to find a sense of mystery and wonder lying behind immediate material reality. This hunger was in part reactive. In his teens Yeats had worshipped his father 'above all men'. John B. Yeats, the portrait-painter, was a brilliant, improvident, passionate, irascible man, very attractive – with his 'beautiful, mischievous head' – and sometimes very turbulent: 'Once he threw me against a picture with such violence that I broke the glass with the back of my head.' That was during an argument about art; but Yeats's father's views on philosophy and religion were equally forceful and contentious. He declared himself a sceptic, enemy of all or any religious belief.

But his son thirsted after the intuitable, after the sacred. As he grew more confident in his arguments with his father, about poetry and painting as well as about religion, he grew more and more convinced that the triumph of scientific thinking in the nineteenth century and its insistence on the precise and the measurable was an aberration. And he looked for and found a validation of these feelings in his sense

Bulben', often cloud-capped, inaccessible-looking, 'encircled by terror'. Below Ben Bulben lies the village of Drumcliff, dominated by the church where the poet's ancestor, John Yeats, was once rector: an assertively Christian place, but also 'full of omens'. To the east, up the swift-flowing Garavogue river, lies Lough Gill, a lake full of islands, of which one is Innisfree. To the south is the mysterious mountain of Knocknarea, one of the 'old sacred places', which the dangerous Queen Maeve of Celtic legend is said to haunt. Not far from these 'conspicuous hills' lie Dromahair, 'cold and vapour-turbaned' Lugnagall, Sleuth Woods, Dooney, where the fiddler played, the well at Tullaghan that Yeats called the Hawk's Well, and 'lonely Echtge of the streams'. This is the fundamental Yeats landscape.

His *Reveries over Childhood and Youth*, a series of autobiographical sketches written in his forties, recalls how his long summers spent among uncles and cousins in Sligo gave the much-displaced child and youth a unique sense of home, of welcome, of acceptance. Even the bad dreams and nightmares he remembers having in that country seem to spring from this strong closeness to the place.

9

of communication with the uncommunicable among the Sligo hills, and among the people he found there.

He would listen to their everyday talk, alive with acceptance of and belief in legend and in a magic that surrounded their everyday lives. He began to write down the stories that these old men and women told, using their daily speech, a speech that quite naturally and unaffectedly echoed with messages from another world.

In his early twenties Yeats began to publish collections of these tales, the best known being *The Celtic Twilight* (1893), much quoted in this book. And in these fresh narratives, full of 'the talk of hen-wives and queer old men', Yeats claimed to be describing accurately otherworldly manifestations that he had heard of and sometimes seen for himself; his 'dhouls and fairies' are presented in the most matter-of-fact way.

He knew that the fairies, the Sidhe, the Tuatha de Danaan were a serious matter. They were demi-urges, cosmic forces active below the surface of life. In a more prosaic sense they were projections of everyday fears and hopes of a culture of poverty: disappearing children, stricken wives, lost husbands, withered crops, sick animals, illness, feeble-mindedness, insanity, death – if these could be blamed on the fairies, it was a way of coping. Or, in the recurring vision of a Tir na nOg – a land of eternal youth, 'a palace of white marble, amid orange trees', full of delight and gaiety – the fairies provided a way of hoping. But beyond that there was the haunted air, the almost tangible presence of the 'other', at once enticing and inimical, and very moving and exciting for Yeats.

> The things a man has heard and seen are threads of life, and if he pull them carefully from the confused distaff of memory, any who will can weave them into whatever garment of belief pleases them best. I too have woven my garment like another . . .

Searching always for richer answers to life's overwhelming questions, he wove many such garments of belief. The world of Faery furnished one, and through the years he looked for answers in the occult, in the esoteric, in the practice of magic, and even in the revelations of automatic writing. If we cast a cold late-twentieth-century eye over this, much of it now seems eccentric, even foolish. Yet the wise poems that emerge from these explorations persuade us to accept them as

stratagems, ways to express a 'mental atmosphere'. Yeats often insisted that his poems were about moods, not about ideas. It seems wise to take him at his word.

At the heart of all the poet's writing lies an intuition that everyday life, ordinary existence, is not all that is on offer. There are exciting moments, or it is possible to *create* exciting moments, which take us beyond the ordinary; moments when one is in contact with another order of being, when one can speak about life in a dramatically different way. In both life and art he strove to be a visionary. His frequent impulse was to turn away from the material world that seemed so temporary, so provisional to him. A conflict naturally arose here. His mystical position – 'Let all things pass away' – contrasted sharply with the immediacy of his involvement in the here and now. But such conflicts were at the heart of his psyche and are the life-blood of his poetry. His transcendent visions rest firmly on physical realities

> *I bend my body to the spade*
> *Or grope with a dirty hand.*

So in 'The Man who Dreamed of Faeryland', an early poem that wanders all over Sligo, fairy wonders abound. But Yeats conveys through these visionary excursions a strong sense of real life, what can be found there, what can be bitterly missed. Again, in 'The Host of the Air', the lean simplicity and delicacy of its ballad rhythms

> And he saw young men and young girls
> Who danced on a level place,
> And Bridget his bride among them,
> With a sad and a gay face

catch the seriousness of Irish folk-themes – life's dangerousness, precariousness, the pathos of human loss.

Similarly, his later idealised vision of an extra-corporeal Byzantium must confront the pulsing reality of

> The young
> In one another's arms, birds in the trees
> – Those dying generations – at their song,
> The salmon-falls, the mackerel-crowded seas,
> Fish, flesh, or fowl, commend all summer long
> Whatever is begotten, born, and dies.

'The Lake Isle of Innisfree' notwithstanding, Yeats was never an escapist. He had no use for private poetry. 'All that's personal soon rots; it must be packed with salt.' The salt came from discourse with the world; he wanted 'to speak out of the people to the people'. His enthusiastic interest in Irish folklore was a function also of his active interest in Irish nationalistic politics. For the Irish literary revival was for many years part of an Irish political revival. All through the time that Yeats was collecting and editing Sligo folk-tales he was also forming societies, chairing meetings, reviewing books and making speeches, leading a strenuous life of dedication to the establishment of an Irish national literary awareness, inseparable from a political awareness, with a loyalty that sometimes, as he admits engagingly, could approach self-deception:

> We . . . paid great honour to the Irish poets who wrote in English, and quoted them in our speeches . . . I knew in my heart that the most of them wrote badly, and yet such romance clung about them, such a desire for Irish poetry was in all our minds, that I kept on saying, not only to others but to myself, that most of them wrote well, or all but well.

Yeats is remembering evenings with the Young Ireland Society, a political and cultural movement of long standing, which had romantic nationalist learnings. There he had met John O'Leary – 'His long imprisonment, his longer banishment, his magnificent head, his scholarship, his pride, his integrity, all that aristocratic dream nourished amid little shops and little farms' – O'Leary's passionate but measured faith in Irish political activism and in Irish writing deepened Yeats's sense of a cultural identity, and pushed him to link politics with art. Soon he was announcing himself as poet and patriot:

> Know, that I would accounted be
> True brother of a company
> That sang, to sweeten Ireland's wrong,
> Ballad and story, rann and song . . .

And so active had he become in the maelstrom of nationalist politics by the turn of the century that he even earned a confidential police report: 'William Butler Yeats – a literary enthusiast, more or less a revolutionary.'

Yeats was no revolutionary; he had mixed feelings about the 'fanatic heart'. But he certainly had friends who advocated violent solutions, notably two women, Constance Gore-Booth and Maud Gonne. Maud Gonne was to become a lifelong obsession for Yeats. He first met Constance in 1894 at Lissadell, a large late-Georgian house in beautiful grounds running alongside the waters of Sligo Bay. The family had lived on this spot since the early eighteenth century (and, in fact, still do). Constance, then a young and strikingly beautiful woman, known after her marriage as the Countess Markievicz, was a fiercely dedicated participant in the national struggle.

Constance was very attractive to Yeats, as both aristocrat and revolutionary. But not long after that first meeting at Lissadell he began to move in a different literary and political direction, shifting his 'place' from Sligo to Galway. In literary Dublin in 1897 he met Lady Augusta Gregory, ardent patron of Irish Arts. This meeting and his meeting at about the same time with the playwright J.M. Synge had a profound influence on the poet's life and work.

Lady Augusta Gregory.
In 1909 Yeats wrote 'She
has been to me mother,
friend, sister and brother.'

Coole Park in Lady Gregory's day.

COOLE PARK

In 1897 Yeats made his first visit to the fine eighteenth-century Gregory mansion at Coole Park in County Galway. He spent many subsequent summers there. Lady Gregory, a widow, came, like the Gore-Booths, from Ascendancy stock; she shared many of the political views of the Anglo-Irish landlord class and was as content to live off her rent-roll as any other owner of a Great House. But she was also an avid cultural nationalist, gathering folk tales in Galway much as Yeats had done in Sligo. She was beginning to write plays about the local peasantry, and had developed some sympathies with Irish nationalist causes. For a while she became in effect Yeats's patron, and as he was now writing plays himself the two began a literary collaboration.

Together with Edward Martyn, an Irish Catholic landlord who lived in nearby Tulira Castle and who also wrote plays, they began discussions that eventually led to the founding of the Irish National Theatre Society. In 1904, amidst some excitement, the Abbey Theatre was born and Lady Gregory's one-act comedies, Yeats's verse-plays and now the work of J.M. Synge were produced there. Yeats became involved in 'theatre business, management of men'.

Coole Park became Yeats's centre of image-making, his 'place', much as Sligo had been in his twenties and early thirties. Exhausted by the complex pressures and bickerings of literary and political

Dublin, he loved to come to the ordered life of Lady Gregory's house, its fine library, its 'levelled lawns and gravelled ways'. He had already seen something of this kind of privileged Irish life at Lissadell. Great Houses now become for him homes of 'high laughter, loveliness and ease', where, he believed (or chose to believe), 'passion and precision have been one'.

Coole Park's 'traditional sanctity and loveliness', had immense appeal and he had no difficulty in contrasting those gardens, the lake with its wild swans and the house's calm, confident, patrician lifestyle with the drabness and rootlessness of modern urban living, where 'We shift about . . . like some poor Arab tribesman and his tent.'

Although he liked occasionally to dwell on the nobility of his Butler forebears, Yeats was not an aristocrat himself and never very seriously suggested he was. His only claim for his ancestors was that they were 'Merchant and scholar who have left me blood,/That has not passed through any huckster's loin.' Solidly middle-class, in fact, as were the men in Ireland's history whom he most admired: Swift, Berkeley, Burke, Parnell and Grattan. 'We were merchant people of the town. No matter how rich we grew . . . we could never be "county", nor indeed had we any desire to be.' But he could go pretty far, for a man so recently involved in nationalistic and democratic politics, in his defence of the Ascendancy and Anglo-Irish privilege. The Irish Great House, he once asserted, 'called to my mind a life set amid natural beauty and the activities of servants and labourers who themselves seemed natural, as bird and tree are natural.' It is hard to accept now, this vision of underpaid servants and labourers being contentedly bird-like and tree-like. Equally hard to accept then, no doubt. And it is harder still to know, on reading the beautiful poem 'Upon a House shaken by the Land Agitation', that its origin lies in Yeats's concern that government legislation might lower the rents of Coole's tenantry and thus threaten Lady Gregory's leisured way of life.

However, one can suspect some coat-trailing here, as there surely is in a more outspoken and even less acceptable contribution to the defence of a privileged class, which Yeats made in 1909: 'One feels that where all must make their living they will live not for life's sake but the work's, and all will be the poorer.' This sounds like self-parody; or is Maud Gonne's too often quoted remark, 'silly Willy', for once appropriate?

In any case Coole Park and its world undoubtedly exercised a quite noticeable influence on Yeats's politics. One can chart a shift in his concerns away from participation in any kind of levelling nationalistic activities, though by no means any shift away from public life and the desire to influence it. He moved towards a more reactionary, more authoritarian view of things. Later, in his passionate quest for an Order and an Authority to stem the blood-dimmed tide, he flirted briefly with some largely ludicrous yet still dangerous Irish fascist elements. He soon dropped that, but he clung always to his admiration for the Great House tradition. In the last year of his life he wrote the play *Purgatory*, in which he has a central character proclaim:

> to kill a house
> Where great men grew up, married, died,
> I here declare a capital offence.

Extreme stuff. But paradoxically the dubious, even dangerous positions that Yeats sometimes affected (the worst can be found in a late essay 'Tomorrow's Revolution') were mostly a matter of stance, of pose – his famous donning of masks, often enough balanced with contrary ironies. And unquestionably the great Coole Park poems stretch the imagination far beyond any narrow ideological theme. In 'Coole Park, 1929', 'Coole Park and Ballylee, 1931' and the 'Ancestral Houses' section of 'Meditations in Time of Civil War' the Great House is not celebrated simply as a haunt of privilege; it has become a rich source of meditation, full of generosity and visionary depth, as in 'A Prayer for my Daughter':

> And may her bridegroom bring her to a house
> Where all's accustomed, ceremonious;
> For arrogance and hatred are the wares
> Peddled in the thoroughfares.
> How but in custom and in ceremony
> Are innocence and beauty born?
> Ceremony's a name for the rich horn,
> And custom for the spreading laurel tree.

In his heart, Yeats probably knew that the Great House had long outlived its function, and in 'Ancestral Houses' he recognized that fact:

> And maybe the great-grandson of that house,
> For all its bronze and marble, 's but a mouse.

Coole Park is gone now, demolished as Yeats presciently feared it might be, but the woods and park remain, and remain as Yeatsian as Sligo.

THOOR BALLYLEE

Yeats inherited Sligo; Coole Park came as a gift; Thoor Ballylee he fashioned for himself. In 1917 he bought for a song, or, more precisely, for thirty-five pounds, a ruined medieval tower in Ballylee, County Galway. Thoor Ballylee, with its castellated roof, stands beside a mill-stream not far from the small town of Gort. Inside the massive walls its four storeys are joined by a winding stone stairway. Yeats had wanted to buy the tower for years. Apart from the solid richness of its stonework and its superb site among the trees, dominating bridge and river, and apart from the fact that he could see Coole's Seven Woods from its parapets, the tower had links with his earlier interests both in Sligo and at Coole. The village of Ballylee had close associations with Blind Raftery, the renowned eighteenth-century harper. Raftery had sung the praises of the beautiful Mary Hines, a girl whose skin 'was so white it looked blue.' The Sidhe had stolen her for her beauty – a tale Yeats had already told in *The Celtic Twilight*. Lady Gregory had translated the Raftery song . . . Ballylee was already thoroughly Yeatsian.

When Yeats bought the tower, he found a builder – named, by perfect coincidence, Raftery – to repair and restore the place for himself and his new wife. The short dedication poem he then wrote to celebrate its restoration is a declaration of the tower's special importance to him. It was to be the new place and the new symbol of his time-defying art:

> And may these characters remain
> When all is ruin once again.

His work, he announced, was now to be 'rooted in the earth', just as this tower was. Already in the little dedicatory poem the particularity of 'old mill boards and sea-green slates,/And smithy work from the Gort forge . . .' is in this earthy vein, and in much of the poetry that was written over the next fifteen years the spirit of the place is present in the most solid way.

The titles of two volumes published when Yeats was in his sixties, *The Tower* and *The Winding Stair*, proclaim the tower's emblematic importance. Having absorbed and moved beyond his Sligo inheritance, and beyond Coole Park's hospitality, the mature poet has made his own house and has invested it with his own meanings. In 'Blood and the Moon' he announces:

> this tower is my symbol; I declare
> This winding, gyring, spiring treadmill of a stair is my
> ancestral stair. . .

Yeats had *accepted* Coole Park; it was a given, its symbolic meaning already established. But his tower was another matter. On Thoor Ballylee he freely projected a complex of his own contradictory hopes and fears, for himself and for Ireland, and the tower's meanings for him varied with his moods.

In 'Prayer on Going into My House', the place is greeted as a symbol of a life where everything is to be as plain and simple as life 'for shepherd lads in Galilee'. It was to be his own more modest version of Coole Park, a second home, a place to slake the poet's thirst for sober civility:

> grant
> That I myself for portions of the year
> May handle nothing and set eyes on nothing
> But what the great and passionate have used . . .

The solemn grandiosity of those lines is then happily and characteristically relieved by the placing of a smart curse on any future bureaucrat who might dare to meddle with his place: 'Manacle his soul upon the Red Sea bottom'.

Yeats took over the tower's history to make it his own, *his* ancestral tower. In one mood it became, like Coole Park, a symbol of order and continuity. And he invoked distinguished presences from the past as guests, visitors from the rich horn of eighteenth-century Ireland – Swift, Berkeley, Burke and Goldsmith. But in a darker mood he saw the tower as the scene of Ireland's violent history, 'blood-saturated ground', a theatre for the arrogance of power. Its battlements, in their half-ruined, unrestored state, 'half-dead at the top', symbolized the decay of nations in 'this pragmatical, preposterous pig of a world'.

In 1918 Yeats used his tower as the locus for a great elegiac poem to Lady Gregory's only son, Robert, who was a major in the Royal Flying Corps and who had been killed in action over Italy early in the year. The tower becomes a place of retreat for meditation on the deaths of various 'close companions'. Old George Pollexfen, the strange uncle of the poet's childhood and youth, is remembered with wry affection, as is the learned but self-destructive poet Lionel Johnson whom Yeats had known and admired in the 1890s (though, his *Memoirs* tell us, 'the discovery that he drank . . . altered my view of the world'). His tone deepens as he remembers his fellow-worker and close friend from the early Abbey days, 'that enquiring man John Synge', then swells as he sings a song of praise for Lady Gregory's dead son, who had seemed to him a new Renaissance man, 'Our Sidney', with all the virtues and all the gifts – 'Soldier, scholar, horseman he'. 'In Memory of Major Robert Gregory' is a poem of great power and poignancy, written with unaffected simplicity and given a special immediacy by the image that it evokes of the poet sitting alone in his tower, hearing a bitter wind outside that 'shakes the shutter', speaking aloud of old dead friends and driven at last to silence by the thought of his young dead friend.

Yeats's tower could be both destroyer and preserver. In 'A Dialogue of Self and Soul' we toil up Thoor Ballylee's winding stair:

> Set all your mind upon the steep ascent,
> Upon the broken, crumbling battlement,
> Upon the breathless starlit air . . .

to find the tower embodying a quarrel that the sixty-two-year-old poet stages with himself. His soul sees those winding stairs as a pathway to darkness and death, but also beyond death to spiritual liberation, the blessedness of eternity. Then the body fights back with the sword of life and art. There is no victory in this argument; unresolved tension is all. Yet for a moment, in this last view of Yeats's tower, it becomes the setting for the artist's triumphant Blakeian song.

> We must laugh and we must sing,
> We are blest by everything,
> Everything we look upon is blest.

DUBLIN

Yeats was born in Dublin, in Sandymount, and spent a large part of his adult life there. Dublin became the main arena for his extraordinarily wide range of activities. It has been said of him that in that city he lived many lives in one. Side by side with his absorbed poet's life ran an eclectic, eccentric, wholly serious and intensely strenuous life as student and teacher of folklore, as mythologist, as historian, as enthusiast of theosophy and related mystical systems. And besides these and other private enterprises he was an immensely energetic public man, variously a journalist, a literary critic, an impresario, a nationalist politician, a public speaker and eventually, for six years, a senator of the Irish Free State.

Clearly Dublin was another 'place' for Yeats. This book cannot illustrate all the tumultuous years that Yeats spent there. But a glance or two at his life as a schoolboy and student is of interest, together with a look at his tortuous emotional attachments, his growing engagement with figures from Dublin past and his reluctant involvement with figures from Dublin present.

At fifteen, he and his family went to live in Howth, the hilly peninsula that stretches north-east of the city. His *Reveries* gives us a glimpse or two of his early years there: the schoolboy sailing out to Lambay Island, off the north coast, to fish and swim; the adolescent struggling with his awakening sexuality – 'It all came upon me when I was close upon seventeen like the bursting of a shell' – roaming the Hill of Howth on warm spring nights, even sleeping out there among the famous rhododendrons at the castle; the embarrassed, impecunious art student, laughed at for grudging the halfpenny toll that in those days was exacted for crossing the Metal Bridge over the Liffey.

It was as a student in Dublin that Yeats had first met John O'Leary: and at the art college in Kildare Street the poet's adult intellectual life began. He met George Russell (known as 'AE') there; a fellow enthusiast in the Celtic Twilight movement. There is no need to pursue Yeats's plunges with AE into psychic research, esoteric Buddhism, Madame Blavatsky and the setting up of the Dublin Hermetic Society, except to remark that it all began in a room in a York Street tenement, where Yeats's father had his artist's studio, and

John O'Leary, the Fenian leader who fired Yeats's nationalism.

that later Yeats and AE forgathered as Theosophists in the more elegant surroundings of Ely Place.

Dublin was also the scene of Yeats's long, frustrated love for Maud Gonne. He was only twenty-three when he first met her and, as he said, 'the troubling of my life began'. He became obsessed by Maud Gonne and remained so for at least thirty years. The obsession certainly lasted until his marriage at fifty-two, and, judging by the evidence of his poetry, probably continued well beyond that time.

> Maud Gonne at Howth station waiting a train,
> Pallas Athene in that straight back and arrogant head

Maud Gonne, like Constance Gore-Booth, had thrown herself into the Irish nationalist and revolutionary struggle. Like the countess she was strikingly beautiful; unlike her she was not a daughter of the Anglo-Irish Ascendancy; her father was an English army officer. Yeats saw her as brave, wild, wilful, dangerous, a personification of his vision of freedom from life's impositions. When in 1902 she played the heroine in his play about the rebellion of 1798, *Cathleen ni Houlihan*, she seemed the perfect incarnation of this patriotic figure. As she stood tall and valiant on the stage, she appeared to him, he said, in the grandiloquent tones that he not infrequently affected at this time in his life, as 'a divine being fallen into our mortal infirmity'.

15

Maud Gonne in Paris. Yeats wrote 'I had never thought to see in a living woman so great a beauty.'

Yeats was shocked when in 1903 Maud Gonne impulsively married Major John MacBride, later to be described as a 'drunken, vain-glorious lout'. But he continued to write a magnificent series of love poems about her, poems that combine fierce personal feeling with angry political debate and then effortlessly lift off to the level of myth. He celebrated her beauty, 'like a tightened bow', her recklessness and her moral strength. But when he heard, for instance, that she was encouraging tenants to kill their Anglo-Irish landlords in Kerry, he was soon examining his own ambiguous feelings about the simplifications of political commitment and, in the love poems themselves, rehearsing his doubts about revolutionary politics. He loved her, admired her and mistrusted her, feeling in the end that political intransigence had destroyed her.

> She lived in storm and strife,
> Her soul had such desire
> For what proud death may bring
> That it could not endure
> The common good of life,
> But lived as 'twere a king . . .

His conflicting feelings about Maud Gonne and political activism were echoed in his feelings about the city of Dublin itself. Dublin was part of Yeats's Ireland, but it could never be a Sligo or a Coole Park for him. He had many hard words for 'This blind and ignorant town'. During his involvement in the Abbey Theatre in the 1900s he grew increasingly impatient with its middle-class Dublin audiences. Their rejection of the challenges that his, Lady Gregory's and especially Synge's plays offered to their 'soft' nationalism, their contentment with comfortable, sentimental stage-Irishry, enraged him. He grew impatient, too, with the shortcomings he found within the Dublin theatre scene, especially with any tendency towards finding easy solutions to artistic problems – 'the more difficult pleasure is the nobler pleasure'. His daily task of coping with the intricacies of theatre management, at first fascinating to him, grew wearying; in the end he found that it 'rent/Spontaneous joy and natural content/ Out of my heart.'

In 1907 came Synge's *The Playboy of the Western World*, the notorious riots that greeted it and respectable Dublin's decision that the play was 'immoral'. Yeats wrote a fine, angry poem, 'On those that hated "The Playboy of the Western World"'. In the same year the noble old Fenian John O'Leary died. These events, taken with the strong influence of Coole-derived ideas about aristocratic virtue, caused Yeats to move away from active participation in Dublin's democratic political life and encouraged his growing disgust with the city's philistine middle-class – 'the lowest class, morally', O'Leary had called them.

The business of Sir Hugh Lane's paintings especially stirred Yeats's anger. In 1913 Lane, a nephew of Lady Gregory, had offered his fine collection of Impressionist – and, at that date, avant-garde – paintings as a gift to Dublin's Municipal Gallery, if the city would agree to house them properly. Dublin Corporation, strongly influenced by campaigns in the popular press, in effect rejected this splendid challenge – an act that Yeats saw as typical of the new philistinism. His 'September, 1913' contrasts the pious, money-grubbing commercialism of the times with John O'Leary's romantic nationalism; and in another poem, 'To A Wealthy Man', he contrasts with finely controlled indignation the nervous, penny-pinching contribution of a Guinness baron to the Lane fund with the grandeur of a Renaissance prince's open-handed delight in the arts and his proud indifference to vulgar public opinion.

Dublin had now become for him a paradigm of the ruined modern metropolis, where 'meditation is impossible, where action is a mechanical routine, where the chest narrows and the stature sinks'. So he built himself another place in Dublin, a Dublin of the mind, an idealised eighteenth-century city. This was Augustan Dublin, with its celebrated Georgian terraces and squares, spacious and elegant expressions of a society where 'all's accustomed, ceremonious'.

Scorning more and more 'the seeming needs of my fool-driven land', he peopled his city with exemplary figures from the past, worthies monumentally remembered in the city's thoroughfares and public buildings, the eighteenth-century worthies whom he had invited to his tower at Ballylee.

But before these came the nineteenth-century's Parnell, the first victim of cowardly middle-class morality and for Yeats a symbol of cold probity and passion working together. In 'To a Shade', the poet contemplates Parnell's statue in the burial ground at Glasnevin and links him with Hugh Lane, 'a man/Of your own passionate, serving kind'. Both of these public benefactors had been cynically betrayed by the philistines, 'at their old tricks yet'. Yeats praised Parnell at the expense of two other nineteenth-century heroes: Daniel O'Connell, a man honoured in Dublin as the champion of Catholic emancipation, whom Yeats iconoclastically dismissed as a mob-pleaser, the 'great Comedian'; and 'that cringing firbolg' Thomas Moore of the *Irish Melodies*, Dublin's favourite poet, castigated by Yeats as a turncoat Anglicizing versifier. Yeats never lost his interest in Parnell and came back to him towards the end of his life with some rowdy, drinking songs:

> Come gather round me, Parnellites,
> And praise our chosen man;
> Stand upright on your legs a while,
> Stand upright while you can . . .

Yeats had stirred himself in 1913 to support the workers when the great Dublin Lock-out had tried to break the Irish Transport and General Workers' Union – one of those moments in Irish history when almost everyone was pressed to take sides. But his general state of mind in 1916 can be measured by what he wrote to Lady Gregory about his 1913 poem. He treats Ireland as a nation of shopkeepers: 'I described Ireland, if the present intellectual movement failed, as a little greasy huxtering nation.' A low point indeed.

But then came the Easter Rising and the armed occupation of the General Post Office. That extraordinary sacrificial explosion of nationalist feeling against British authority, with all its desperate courage and dedication and all its foolhardiness – that 'delirium of the brave' – stirred Yeats deeply. Romantic Ireland was not dead and gone after all. The doomed insurrection's aftermath, with the shooting by the British of fifteen prisoners, among them two young writers well known to Yeats, moved him to write his celebrated 'Easter 1916', in which the 'casual comedy' of daily Dublin life is 'changed utterly'. The poem concentrates all the ambiguous feelings that Yeats had always had about violent, courageous action; he finds beauty, but a 'terrible' beauty, in these stirring happenings.

Later he remembered the plays he had written glorifying the ancient Irish hero Cuchulain, and recalled that Padraic Pearse, the poet-leader of the Rising, had nurtured an ultra-nationalist Cuchulain cult among some of his followers. He remembered all the years he had spent stimulating nationalist feeling among young literary Irishmen. He also noted that an actor from the Abbey had been the first to die in the fighting at the Post Office. It is not surprising, then, that Yeats, who always believed that poetry should be a public action and that poetry *could* make something happen, grew to feel a weight of responsibility for this moment in history and for the violent deaths of those young men. In one of his very last poems he asks himself whether his play *Cathleen ni Houlihan* might not have sent out 'Certain men the English shot'.

Other 'Rising' poems were to follow. In 'The Statues' (1937) Yeats imagines that Cuchulain himself on that famous occasion 'stalked' the Post Office. The authorities have now erected a statue of Cuchulain there to commemorate the Rising. Dublin became a poet's 'place' for Yeats, but it was mostly a place of statues and monuments, fitting enough in a city that lives so much with its distant and recent past.

In the Thirties Yeats, pursuing Dublin's past, developed further his special interest in those exemplary worthies he had invited to Thoor

Ballylee, the great radical conservatives: Tory Swift, Old-Whig Burke and the idealist philosopher Bishop Berkeley.

Swift he loved for the passionate intensity with which he defended tradition, his savage indignation at mindless change, his prophetic views on the destructiveness of revolution, his dark realism. 'Swift haunts me; he is always just round the next corner.' Yeats felt an affinity with Swift, with his clear-sightedness and courage, even his final craziness: 'He saw civilisation pass from comparative happiness and youthful vigour to an old age of violence and self-contempt.' In 1929, at Coole Park, Yeats translated the Latin epitaph on Swift's monument in St Patrick's Cathedral in Dublin – adding the quintessentially Yeatsian phrase 'world-besotted traveller'. Yeats may have noted with grim amusement that the name of the Dublin burgher who donated the monument is written larger than Swift's own.

Burke deserved his statue at the entrance to Dublin's Trinity College and had earned his place in Yeats's tower for his opposition to England's artificial, commercialised society and for his vision of the state not as a mechanical construct but as organic, a centre of authority that should grow slowly like a forest; Burke had 'proved the state a tree'.

At one time Yeats had dismissed Bishop Berkeley as part of the English colonial presence, but later in life he changed his mind. 'I delight in that fierce young man . . . who . . . established a secret society to examine the philosophy of a neighbouring nation.' He liked it that 'God-appointed' Berkeley had rejected the English philosophers, Newton, Hume and Locke as mechanistic and materialistic, had defined their views in three sentences and 'wrote after each that "we Irish" think otherwise'. He, too, deserved his place in Yeats's Dublin pantheon.

* * *

Yeats was awarded the Nobel Prize for Literature in 1923. A recent winner of the same prize, Joseph Brodsky, has remarked that 'every writing career starts as a personal quest for sainthood, for self-betterment'. Brodsky had Dostoevsky in mind, but his words ring true for Yeats, who was surely, if not a saint, at least a hero of

In his fifties Yeats won the Nobel Prize for Literature.

literature. He was heroic in his intellectual suffering. The story of his life as a poet is one of strenuous makings and breakings, of forging and reforging a language and a style, an unceasing struggle to transform his art and himself. Brodsky went on to say that, as a rule, a man quite soon discovers that his pen accomplishes a lot more than his soul. This, too, is no doubt true of Yeats; yet he was remarkable and heroic in his genuine and impossible struggle to strike a balance between 'perfection of the life or of the work'.

18

He was vulnerable enough, like most modern heroes, and sometimes was laughed at, usually by lesser lights such as his fellow Irish writer George Moore. He took risks and they did not always come off. He could be arrogant and foolish (though arrogance and folly were sometimes marvellously transformed into virtues in his poems) and he could be innocently vain. His poetry is naturally dramatic, and Yeats the man, like Yeats the poet, was often a self-dramatizer, a conscious striker of poses that could balance on the edge of the absurd (his Coole Park defence of the wealthy, for example). Near-comic, too, seem some of his forays into magic, or his adventures with automatic writing, or his apparent gullibilities about life on the astral plane. But he was a very complicated man, and it is surely unwise to pin down too confidently *any* Yeatsian absurdities. Though not precisely witty he had his sense of humour (quietly noticeable in one or two of the autobiographical passages quoted in this book), and his imagination was so volatile that any extreme position was quickly countered with a contrary attitude.

We read him, though, not because he may have been a saint or a hero but because his poetry is exciting. It is exciting first because of that dramatic voice – always full of bite, whether passionate or calm, gay or reckless, or even rascally – and because of the music in that voice. It is exciting because of Yeats's delight in sudden transformations and illuminations, like the curlew's cry on the mountain in 'Paudeen', or the wild swans suddenly 'wheeling in great broken rings' at Coole. The poet's yearning to transcend the body, and his simultaneous delight in the singing and dancing of the senses is exciting. And he is exciting as he broods upon that self that is 'fastened to a dying animal', and as he asks those bewildering questions about body and soul, belief and doubt, youth and age, about love, and about 'the discourtesy of death'. All these questions he throws at us in passionate imagery, offering no solutions, leaving us with only the brilliant, disturbing tensions.

We trust Yeats because although his mind moves quickly towards symbol and myth, it does so without ever losing touch with the object in view. So in 'No Second Troy', a short poem crammed with a confusion of praise and blame, its subject, Maud Gonne, becomes at one moment a violent symbol of Irish revolution, at the next a mythical and noble Helen of Troy, and yet at every moment lives in Yeats's lines as the woman he passionately and despairingly loves.

Yeats's Ireland was put through similar transformations in the poet's tireless pursuit of meaningful symbol and useable myth. The myths and symbols that he elaborated were similarly grounded in the real Ireland:

> All that we did, all that we said or sang
> Must come from contact with the soil . . .

In 'The Man and the Echo', written shortly before he died, he asks that question about *Cathleen ni Houlihan* and the Rising and young men's deaths, questions the responsibilities of art and yet again the meaning of life and death, but gets only a cold sibylline answer from the echo in the rock – 'Lie down and die.' In this last great self-questioning poem Yeats once more makes sure that its intense dialogue is carried on in an exactly identifiable place:

> In a cleft that's christened Alt
> Under broken stone I halt
> At the bottom of a pit
> That broad noon has never lit . . .

Alt is a secret, magical place, a glen high up on the side of Knocknarea in Sligo. Yeats had come back to the place where he had begun. A few months later he died, and in the end they buried him in Sligo, at Drumcliff, under Ben Bulben.

Bernard McCabe

Lough Gill, Sligo.

SLIGO

In a sense Sligo has always been my home.

from *Reveries over Childhood and Youth*

20   Coney Island, from Cummen Strand

A poignant memory came upon me the other day while I was passing the drinking-fountain near Holland Park, for there I and my sister had spoken together of our longing for Sligo and our hatred of London. I know we were both very close to tears and remember with wonder, for I had never known any one that cared for such mementoes, that I longed for a sod of earth from some field I knew, something of Sligo to hold in my hand.

from *Reveries over Childhood and Youth*

The river Garavogue, Sligo Town

THE MEDITATION OF THE OLD FISHERMAN

You waves, though you dance by my feet like children at play,
Though you glow and you glance, though you purr and you dart;
In the Junes that were warmer than these are, the waves were more gay,
When I was a boy with never a crack in my heart.

The herring are not in the tides as they were of old;
My sorrow! for many a creak gave the creel in the cart
That carried the take to Sligo town to be sold,
When I was a boy with never a crack in my heart.

And ah, you proud maiden, you are not so fair when his oar
Is heard on the water, as they were, the proud and apart.
Who paced in the eve by the nets on the pebbly shore,
When I was a boy with never a crack in my heart.

Sligo Quay

25

Rosses is a little sea-dividing, sandy plain, covered with short grass, like a green table-cloth, and lying in the foam midway between the round cairn-headed Knocknarea and 'Ben Bulben, famous for hawks':

> But for Ben Bulben and Knocknarea
> Many a poor sailor'd be cast away,

as the rhyme goes.

At the northern corner of Rosses is a little promontory of sand and rocks and grass: a mournful, haunted place. Few countrymen would fall asleep under its low cliff, for he who sleeps here may wake 'silly', the Sidhe having carried off his soul. There is no more ready short-cut to the dim kingdom than this plovery headland.

from *The Celtic Twilight*

Ben Bulben, from Rosses Point

At Sligo, where I still went for my holidays, I stayed with my uncle, George Pollexfen, who had come from Ballina to fill the place of my grandfather, who had retired. My grandfather had no longer his big house, his partner William Middleton was dead, and there had been legal trouble. He was no longer the rich man he had been, and his sons and daughters were married and scattered. He had a tall, bare house overlooking the harbour, and had nothing to do but work himself into a rage if he saw a mudlighter mismanaged or judged from the smoke of a steamer that she was burning cheap coal, and to superintend the making of his tomb.

from *Reveries over Youth and Childhood*

Once when staying with my uncle at Rosses Point, where he went for certain months of the year, I called upon my cousin toward midnight and asked him to get his yacht out, for I wanted to find what sea-birds began to stir before dawn . . . I had wanted the birds' cries for the poem that became fifteen years afterwards 'The Shadowy Waters' . . . I had found again the windy light that moved me when a child.

from *Reveries over Youth and Childhood*

George Pollexfen's house, Sligo Town

At the place, close to the Dead Man's Point, at the Rosses, where the disused pilot-house looks out to sea through two round windows like eyes, a mud cottage stood in the last century. It also was a watchhouse, for a certain old Michael Bruen, who had been a smuggler, and was still the father and grandfather of smugglers, lived there, and when, after nightfall, a tall French schooner crept over the bay from Roughley, it was his business to hang a horn lantern in the southern window, that the news might travel to Dorren's Island, and thence by another horn lantern, to the village of the Rosses.

from *The Secret Rose*

The Pilot House, near Elsinore, Rosses Point

Drumcliff and Rosses were, are, and ever shall be, please Heaven! places of unearthly resort. I have lived near by them and in them, time after time, and thereby gathered much faery lore. Drumcliff is a wide green valley, lying at the foot of Ben Bulben, whereon the great Saint Columba himself, the builder of many of the old ruins in the valley, climbed one day to get near Heaven with his prayers . . .

Drumcliff is a great place for omens. Before a prosperous fishing season a herring-barrel appears in the midst of a storm-cloud; and at a place called Columcille's Strand, a place of marsh and mire, an ancient boat, with Saint Columba himself, comes floating in from sea on a moonlight night; a portent of a brave harvesting. They have their dread portents too. Some few seasons ago a fisherman saw, far on the horizon, renowned Hy Brazil, where he who touches shall find no more labour or care, nor cynic laughter, but shall go walking about under shadiest boscage, and enjoy the conversation of Cuchulain and his heroes. A vision of Hy Brazil forebodes national troubles.

Drumcliff and Rosses are choke-full of ghosts. By bog, road, rath, hillside, sea-border they gather in all shapes: headless women, men in armour, shadow hares, fire-tongued hounds, whistling seals, and so on.

from *The Celtic Twilight*

Drumcliff Church, where Yeats is buried

THE LAKE ISLE OF INNISFREE

I will arise and go now, and go to Innisfree,
And a small cabin build there, of clay and wattles made:
Nine bean-rows will I have there, a hive for the honey-bee,
And live alone in the bee-loud glade.

And I shall have some peace there, for peace comes dropping slow,
Dropping from the veils of the morning to where the cricket sings;
There midnight's all a glimmer, and noon a purple glow,
And evening full of the linnet's wings.

I will arise and go now, for always night and day
I hear lake water lapping with low sounds by the shore;
While I stand on the roadway, or on the pavements grey,
I hear it in the deep heart's core.

The Isle of Innisfree

In a cleft that's christened Alt
Under broken stone I halt
At the bottom of a pit
That broad noon has never lit,
And shout a secret to the stone.
All that I have said and done,
Now that I am old and ill,
Turns into a question till
I lie awake night after night
And never get the answers right.

from *The Man and the Echo*

The Glen at Alt, Knocknarea

TOWARDS BREAK OF DAY

Was it the double of my dream
The woman that by me lay
Dreamed, or did we halve a dream
Under the first cold gleam of day?

I thought: 'There is a waterfall
Upon Ben Bulben side
That all my childhood counted dear;
Were I to travel far and wide
I could not find a thing so dear.'
My memories had magnified
So many times childish delight.

I would have touched it like a child
But knew my finger could but have touched
Cold stone and water. I grew wild,
Even accusing Heaven because
It had set down among its laws:
Nothing that we love over-much
Is ponderable to our touch.

I dreamed towards break of day,
The cold blown spray in my nostril.
But she that beside me lay
Had watched in bitterer sleep
The marvellous stag of Arthur,
That lofty white stag, leap
From mountain steep to steep.

Glencar Waterfall, Ben Bulben

Many of the tales in this book were told me by one Paddy Flynn, a little bright-eyed old man, who lived in a leaky and one-roomed cabin in the village of Ballisodare, which is, he was wont to say, 'the most gentle' – whereby he meant faery – 'place in the whole of County Sligo.' Others hold it, however, but second to Drumcliff and Dromahair. The first time I saw him he was bent above the fire with a can of mushrooms at his side; the next time he was asleep under a hedge, smiling in his sleep. He was indeed always cheerful, though I thought I could see in his eyes (swift as the eyes of a rabbit, when they peered out of their wrinkled holes) a melancholy which was wellnigh a portion of their joy; the visionary melancholy of purely instinctive natures and of all animals.

from *The Celtic Twilight*

Left: Ballisodare
Right: Pollexfen's mill, Owenmore river, Ballisodare

RED HANRAHAN'S SONG ABOUT IRELAND

The old brown thorn-trees break in two high over Cummen Strand,
Under a bitter black wind that blows from the left hand;
Our courage breaks like an old tree in a black wind and dies,
But we have hidden in our hearts the flame out of the eyes
Of Cathleen, the daughter of Houlihan.

The wind has bundled up the clouds high over Knocknarea,
And thrown the thunder on the stones for all that Maeve can say.
Angers that are like noisy clouds have set our hearts abeat;
But we have all bent low and low and kissed the quiet feet
Of Cathleen, the daughter of Houlihan.

The yellow pool has overflowed high up on Clooth-na-Bare,
For the wet winds are blowing out of the clinging air;
Like heavy flooded waters our bodies and our blood;
But purer than a tall candle before the Holy Rood
Is Cathleen, the daughter of Houlihan.

42   Pilot House, Coney Island and Ox Mountains

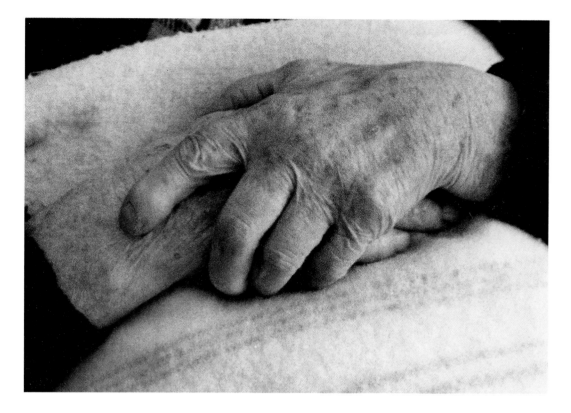

They had hands like claws, and their knees
Were twisted like the old thorn-trees
By the waters.
I heard the old, old men say,
'All that's beautiful drifts away
Like the waters.'

from *The Old Men Admiring Themselves in the Water*

Glencar Lake

'Memory Harbour', Rosses Point

When I look at my brother's picture, 'Memory Harbour' – houses and anchored ship and distant lighthouse all set close together as in some old map – I recognise in the blue-coated man with the mass of white shirt the pilot I went fishing with, and I am full of disquiet and of excitement, and I am melancholy because I have not made more and better verses.

from *Reveries over Childhood and Youth*

46

A Fiddler at Dooney

THE FIDDLER OF DOONEY

When I play on my fiddle in Dooney,
Folk dance like a wave of the sea;
My cousin is priest in Kilvarnet,
My brother in Mocharabuiee.

I passed my brother and cousin:
They read in their books of prayer;
I read in my book of songs
I bought at the Sligo fair.

When we come at the end of time
To Peter sitting in state,
He will smile on the three old spirits,
But call me first through the gate;

For the good are always the merry,
Save by an evil chance,
And the merry love the fiddle,
And the merry love to dance:

And when the folk there spy me,
They will all come up to me,
With 'Here is the fiddler of Dooney!'
And dance like a wave of the sea.

I know you now, for long ago
I met you on a cloudy hill
Beside old thorn trees and a well.

from *The Only Jealousy of Emer*

The Hawk's Well (Tullaghan), near Coolaney

Where the wave of moonlight glosses
The dim grey sands with light,
Far off by furthest Rosses
We foot it all the night,
Weaving olden dances,
Mingling hands and mingling glances
Till the moon has taken flight;
To and fro we leap
And chase the frothy bubbles,
While the world is full of troubles
And is anxious in its sleep.
Come away, O human child!
To the waters and the wild
With a faery, hand in hand,
For the world's more full of weeping than you can understand.

from *The Stolen Child*

Sunset over Rosses Point

A little north of the town of Sligo, on the southern side of Ben Bulben, some hundreds of feet above the plain, is a small white square in the limestone. No mortal has ever touched it with his hand; no sheep or goat has ever browsed grass beside it. There is no more inaccessible place upon the earth, and to an anxious consideration few more encircled by terror. It is the door of Faeryland. In the middle of night it swings open, and the unearthly troop rushes out . . . Sometimes a new-wed bride or a new-born baby goes with them into their mountains; the door swings to behind, and the new-born or the new-wed moves henceforth in the bloodless land of Faery; happy, the story has it, but doomed to melt at the Last Judgment like bright vapour, for the soul cannot live without sorrow. Through this door of white stone, and the other doors of that land where *geabheadh tu an sonas aer pingin* ('you can buy joy for a penny'), have gone those kings, queens, and princes whose stories are in our old Gaelic literature.

from *The Celtic Twilight*

Limestone markings on Ben Bulben

Where the wandering water gushes
From the hills above Glen-Car,
In pools among the rushes
That scarce could bathe a star,
We seek for slumbering trout
And whispering in their ears
Give them unquiet dreams;
Leaning softly out
From ferns that drop their tears
Over the young streams.
Come away, O human child!
To the waters and the wild
With a faery, hand in hand,
For the world's more full of weeping than you can understand.

from The Stolen Child

Glencar Lake

My old Mayo woman told me one day that something very bad had come down the road and gone into the house opposite, and though she would not say what it was, I knew quite well. Another day she told me of two friends of hers who had been made love to by one whom they believed to be the Devil. One of them was standing by the roadside when he came by on horseback, and asked her to mount up behind him, and go riding. When she would not he vanished. The other was out on the road late at night waiting for her young man, when something came flapping and rolling along the road up to her feet. It had the likeness of a newspaper, and presently it flapped up into her face, and she knew by the size of it that it was the *Irish Times* All of a sudden it changed into a young man, who asked her to go walking with him. She would not, and he vanished.

I know of an old man too, on the slopes of Ben Bulben, who found the Devil ringing a bell under his bed, and he went off and stole the chapel bell and rang him out.

from *The Celtic Twilight*

Ben Bulben

TO A CHILD DANCING IN THE WIND

Dance there upon the shore;
What need have you to care
For wind or water's roar?
And tumble out your hair
That the salt drops have wet;
Being young you have not known
The fool's triumph, nor yet
Love lost as soon as won,
Nor the best labourer dead
And all the sheaves to bind.
What need have you to dread
The monstrous crying of wind?

Strandhill Beach

THE HOSTING OF THE SIDHE

The host is riding from Knocknarea
And over the grave of Clooth-na-Bare;
Caoilte tossing his burning hair,
And Niamh calling *Away, come away:*
Empty your heart of its mortal dream.
The winds awaken, the leaves whirl round,
Our cheeks are pale, our hair is unbound,
Our breasts are heaving, our eyes are agleam,
Our arms are waving, our lips are apart;
And if any gaze on our rushing band,
We come between him and the deed of his hand,
We come between him and the hope of his heart.
The host is rushing 'twixt night and day,
And where is there hope or deed as fair?
Caoilte tossing his burning hair,
And Niamh calling *Away, come away.*

Stone Age site at Carrowmore, Knocknarea

The light of evening, Lissadell,
Great windows open to the south,
Two girls in silk kimonos, both
Beautiful, one a gazelle.
But a raving autumn shears
Blossom from the summer's wreath;
The older is condemned to death,
Pardoned, drags out lonely years
Conspiring among the ignorant.
I know not what the younger dreams –
Some vague Utopia – and she seems,
When withered old and skeleton-gaunt,
An image of such politics.
Many a time I think to seek
One or the other out and speak
Of that old Georgian mansion, mix
Pictures of the mind, recall
That table and the talk of youth,
Two girls in silk kimonos, both
Beautiful, one a gazelle.

from *In Memory of Eva Gore-Booth and Con Markiewicz*

In my childhood I had seen on clear days
from the hill above my grandmother's house
or from the carriage if our drive was towards
Ben Bulben or from the smooth grass hill of
Rosses the grey stone walls of Lissadell
among its trees. We were merchant people
of the town. No matter how rich we grew, no
matter how many thousands a year our mills
or our ships brought in, we could never be
'county', nor indeed had we any desire to
be so.   from *Memoirs*

Lissadell House, home of the Gore-Booths   65

I thought that having conquered bodily desire and the inclination of my mind towards women and love, I should live, as Thoreau lived, seeking wisdom. There was a story in the county history of a tree that had once grown upon that island guarded by some terrible monster and borne the food of the gods. A young girl pined for the fruit and told her lover to kill the monster and carry the fruit away. He did as he had been told, but tasted the fruit; and when he reached the mainland where she had waited for him, he was dying of its powerful virtue. And from sorrow and from remorse she too ate of it and died. I do not remember whether I chose the island because of its beauty or for the story's sake, but I was twenty-two or three before I gave up the dream.

from *Reveries over Childhood and Youth*

Church Island, Lough Gill

He slept under the hill of Lugnagall;
And might have known at last unhaunted sleep
Under that cold and vapour-turbaned steep,
Now that the earth had taken man and all:
Did not the worms that spired about his bones
Proclaim with that unwearied, reedy cry
That God has laid His fingers on the sky,
That from those fingers glittering summer runs
Upon the dancer by the dreamless wave.
Why should those lovers that no lovers miss
Dream, until God burn Nature with a kiss?
The man has found no comfort in the grave.

from *The Man who Dreamed of Faeryland*

Lugnagall Hill, near Glencar Lake

For years to come it was in my thought, as in much of my writing, to seek also to bring again into imaginative life the old sacred places – Slievenamon, Knocknarea – all that old reverence that hung – above all – about conspicuous hills. But I wished by my writings and those of the school I hoped to found to have a secret symbolical relation to these mysteries, for in that way, I thought, there will be a greater richness, a greater claim upon the love of the soul, doctrine without exhortation and rhetoric. Should not religion hide within the work of art as God is within His world, and how can the interpreter do more than whisper? I did not wish to compose rites as if for the theatre. They must in their main outline be the work of invisible hands.

from *Memoirs*

Above: Queen Maeve's Burial Mound, Knocknarea
Right: Knocknarea

I told him I was going to walk round Lough Gill and sleep in a wood. I did not tell him all my object, for I was nursing a new ambition. My father had read to me some passage out of *Walden*, and I planned to live some day in a cottage on a little island called Innisfree, and Innisfree was opposite Slish Wood where I meant to sleep. . . .

I set out from Sligo about six in the evening walking slowly, for it was an evening of great beauty; but though I was well into Slish Wood by bed-time, I could not sleep, not from the discomfort of the dry rock I had chosen for my bed, but from my fear of the wood-ranger. Somebody had told me, though I do not think it could have been true, that he went his round at some unknown hour. I kept going over what I should say if found and could not think of anything he would believe. However, I could watch my island in the early dawn and notice the order of the cries of the birds.

from *Reveries over Childhood and Youth*

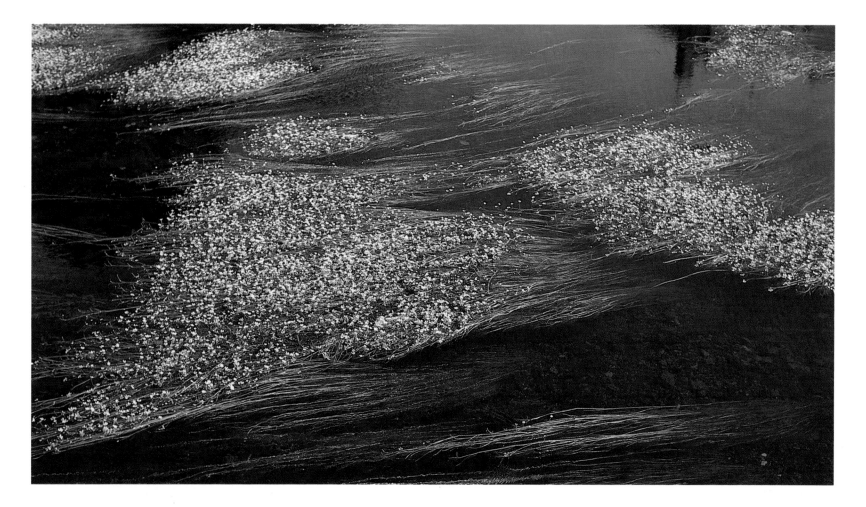

DOWN BY THE SALLEY GARDENS

Down by the salley gardens my love and I did meet;
She passed the salley gardens with little snow-white feet.
She bid me take love easy, as the leaves grow on the tree;
But I, being young and foolish, with her would not agree.

In a field by the river my love and I did stand,
And on my leaning shoulder she laid her snow-white hand.
She bid me take life easy, as the grass grows on the weirs;
But I was young and foolish, and now am full of tears.

Above: Grasses in the weir, Garavogue river
Left: Sallows growing alongside the river

COOLE PARK

I found at last what I had been seeking always, a life of order and of labour, where all outward things were the image of an inward life.

from *The Trembling of the Veil*

Avenue of Ilex trees, Coole Park

IN THE SEVEN WOODS

I have heard the pigeons of the Seven Woods
Make their faint thunder, and the garden bees
Hum in the lime-tree flowers; and put away
The unavailing outcries and the old bitterness
That empty the heart. I have forgot awhile
Tara uprooted, and new commonness
Upon the throne and crying about the streets
And hanging its paper flowers from post to post,
Because it is alone of all things happy.
I am contented, for I know that Quiet
Wanders laughing and eating her wild heart
Among pigeons and bees, while that Great Archer,
Who but awaits His hour to shoot, still hangs
A cloudy quiver over Pairc-na-Lee.

The Seven Woods in the late autumn light

UPON A HOUSE SHAKEN BY THE LAND AGITATION

How should the world be luckier if this house,
Where passion and precision have been one
Time out of mind, became too ruinous
To breed the lidless eye that loves the sun?
And the sweet laughing eagle thoughts that grow
Where wings have memory of wings, and all
That comes of the best knit to the best? Although
Mean roof-trees were the sturdier for its fall,
How should their luck run high enough to reach
The gifts that govern men, and after these
To gradual Time's last gift, a written speech
Wrought of high laughter, loveliness and ease?

The stables, Coole Park

Horses grazing at the lake's edge

THE WILD SWANS AT COOLE

The trees are in their autumn beauty,
The woodland paths are dry,
Under the October twilight the water
Mirrors a still sky;
Upon the brimming water among the stones
Are nine-and-fifty swans.

The nineteenth autumn has come upon me
Since I first made my count;
I saw, before I had well finished,
All suddenly mount
And scatter wheeling in great broken rings
Upon their clamorous wings.

I have looked upon those brilliant creatures,
And now my heart is sore.
All's changed since I, hearing at twilight,
The first time on this shore,
The bell-beat of their wings above my head,
Trod with a lighter tread.

Unwearied still, lover by lover,
They paddle in the cold
Companionable streams or climb the air;
Their hearts have not grown old;
Passion or conquest, wander where they will,
Attend upon them still.

But now they drift on the still water,
Mysterious, beautiful;
Among what rushes will they build,
By what lake's edge or pool
Delight men's eyes when I awake some day
To find they have flown away?

Wild swans at Coole

Here, traveller, scholar, poet, take your stand
When all those rooms and passages are gone,
When nettles wave upon a shapeless mound
And saplings root among the broken stone,
And dedicate – eyes bent upon the ground,
Back turned upon the brightness of the sun
And all the sensuality of the shade –
A moment's memory to that laurelled head.

Steps which once led to Lady Gregory's house,
destroyed in 1941

from *Coole Park, 1929*

One day I was walking over a bit of marshy ground close to Inchy Wood when I felt, all of a sudden, and only for a second, an emotion which I said to myself was the root of Christian mysticism. There had swept over me a sense of weakness, of dependence on a great personal Being somewhere far off yet near at hand. No thought of mine had prepared me for this emotion, for I had been preoccupied with Aengus and Edain, and with Manannan, Son of the Sea. That night I awoke lying upon my back and hearing a voice speaking above me and saying, 'No human soul is like any other human soul, and therefore the love of God for any human soul is infinite, for no other soul can satisfy the same need in God.'

from *The Celtic Twilight*

Inchy Wood, Coole Park

THOOR BALLYLEE

I declare this tower is my symbol; I declare

This winding, gyring, spiring treadmill of a stair is my ancestral stair. . . .

from Blood and the Moon

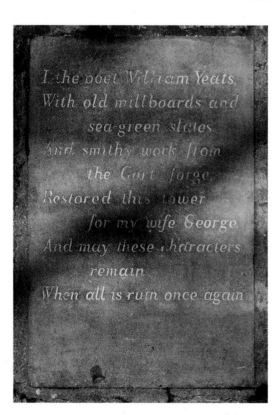

Right: Thoor Ballylee, Co. Galway, Yeats's summer home from 1919–29

Above: The stone inscription was not carved until 1948

A Prayer on Going into My House

God grant a blessing on this tower and cottage
And on my heirs, if all remain unspoiled,
No table or chair or stool not simple enough
For shepherd lads in Galilee; and grant
That I myself for portions of the year
May handle nothing and set eyes on nothing
But what the great and passionate have used
Throughout so many varying centuries
We take it for the norm; yet should I dream
Sinbad the sailor's brought a painted chest,
Or image, from beyond the Loadstone Mountain,
That dream is a norm; and should some limb of the Devil
Destroy the view by cutting down an ash
That shades the road, or setting up a cottage
Planned in a government office, shorten his life,
Manacle his soul upon the Red Sea bottom.

Looking down upon Ballylee

I summon to the winding ancient stair;
Set all your mind upon the steep ascent,
Upon the broken, crumbling battlement,
Upon the breathless starlit air,
Upon the star that marks the hidden pole;
Fix every wandering thought upon
That quarter where all thought is done:
Who can distinguish darkness from the soul?

from *A Dialogue of Self and Soul*

An ancient bridge, and a more ancient tower,
A farmhouse that is sheltered by its wall,
An acre of stony ground,
Where the symbolic rose can break in flower,
Old ragged elms, old thorns innumerable,
The sound of the rain or sound
Of every wind that blows;
The stilted water-hen
Crossing stream again
Scared by the splashing of a dozen cows;

A winding stair, a chamber arched with stone,
A grey stone fireplace with an open hearth,
A candle and written page.
Il Penseroso's Platonist toiled on
In some like chamber, shadowing forth
How the daemonic rage
Imagined everything.
Benighted travellers
From markets and from fairs
Have seen his midnight candle glimmering.

from *Meditations in Time of Civil War*

Blessed be this place,
More blessed still this tower;
A bloody, arrogant power
Rose out of the race
Uttering, mastering it,
Rose like these walls from these
Storm-beaten cottages –
In mockery I have set
A powerful emblem up,
And sing it rhyme upon rhyme
In mockery of a time
Half dead at the top.

from *Blood and the Moon*

Storm-beaten cottage and Tower

Now that we're almost settled in our house
I'll name the friends that cannot sup with us
Beside a fire of turf in th' ancient tower,
And having talked to some late hour
Climb up the narrow winding stair to bed:
Discoverers of forgotten truth
Or mere companions of my youth,
All, all are in my thoughts to-night being dead.

from *In Memory of Major Robert Gregory*

'A grey stone fireplace with an open hearth'

LAND OF HEART'S DESIRE

'I AM OF IRELAND'

'I am of Ireland,
And the Holy Land of Ireland,
And time runs on,' cried she.
'Come out of charity,
Come dance with me in Ireland.'

Burial site at the ancient monastic centre of Clonmacnois, Co. Offaly

The stone fort of Dún Aengus on the south-west coast of Inishmore

And that enquiring man John Synge comes next,
That dying chose the living world for text
And never could have rested in the tomb
But that, long travelling, he had come
Towards nightfall upon certain set apart
In a most desolate stony place,
Towards nightfall upon a race
Passionate and simple like his heart.

from *In Memory of Major Robert Gregory*

Kilronan town, Inishmore, the largest of the Aran Islands

The hour before dawn and the moon covered up;

The little village of Abbey is covered up;

The little narrow trodden way that runs

From the white road to the Abbey of Corcomroe

Is covered up; and all about the hills

Are like a circle of agate or of jade.

Somewhere among great rocks on the scarce grass

Birds cry, they cry their loneliness.

Even the sunlight can be lonely here,

Even hot noon is lonely.

from *The Dreaming of The Bones*

Previous page: Sunset over Inishmore
Above: Recumbent statue of Conor O'Brien, d. 1267
Right: Corcomroe Abbey, the Burren, Co. Clare

I said: [to J.M. Synge] 'Give up Paris. You will never create anything by reading Racine, and Arthur Symons will always be a better critic of French literature. Go to the Aran Islands. Live there as if you were one of the people themselves; express a life that has never found expression.' I had just come from Aran, and my imagination was full of those grey islands where men must reap with knives because of the stones.

He went to Aran and became a part of its life, living upon salt fish and eggs, talking Irish for the most part, but listening also to the beautiful English which has grown up in Irish-speaking districts, and takes its vocabulary from the time of Malory and of the translators of the Bible, but its idiom and its vivid metaphor from Irish.

from the Preface to J.M. Synge's *'The Well of the Saints'*

Rebuilding the storm-damaged walls, Inishmore

I fasted for some forty days on bread and buttermilk,
For passing round the bottle with girls in rags or silk,
In country shawl or Paris cloak, had put my wits astray,
And what's the good of women, for all that they can say
Is fol de rol de rolly O.

Round Lough Derg's holy island I went upon the stones,
I prayed at all the Stations upon my marrow-bones,
And there I found an old man, and though I prayed all day
And that old man beside me, nothing would he say
But fol de rol de rolly O.

from *The Pilgrim*

Lough Derg, Co. Donegal, one of Ireland's most important places of pilgrimage

The July race meeting at Ballybrit, Co. Galway

AT GALWAY RACES

There where the course is,
Delight makes all of the one mind,
The riders upon the galloping horses,
The crowd that closes in behind:
We, too, had good attendance once,
Hearers and hearteners of the work;
Aye, horsemen for companions,
Before the merchant and the clerk
Breathed on the world with timid breath.
Sing on: somewhere at some new moon,
We'll learn that sleeping is not death,
Hearing the whole earth change its tune,
Its flesh being wild, and it again
Crying aloud as the racecourse is,
And we find hearteners among men
That ride upon horses.

THE WITHERING OF THE BOUGHS ·

I cried when the moon was murmuring to the birds:
'Let peewit call and curlew cry where they will,
I long for your merry and tender and pitiful words,
For the roads are unending, and there is no place to my mind.'
The honey-pale moon lay low on the sleepy hill,
And I fell asleep upon lonely Echtge of streams.
No boughs have withered because of the wintry wind;
The boughs have withered because I have told them my dreams.

I know of the leafy paths that the witches take
Who come with their crowns of pearl and their spindles of wool,
And their secret smile, out of the depths of the lake;
I know where a dim moon drifts, where the Danaan kind
Wind and unwind their dances when the light grows cool
On the island lawns, their feet where the pale foam gleams.
No boughs have withered because of the wintry wind;
The boughs have withered because I have told them my dreams.

I know of the sleepy country, where swans fly round
Coupled with golden chains, and sing as they fly.
A king and a queen are wandering there, and the sound
Has made them so happy and hopeless, so deaf and so blind
With wisdom, they wander till all the years have gone by;
I know, and the curlew and peewit on Echtge of streams.
No boughs have withered because of the wintry wind;
The boughs have withered because I have told them my dreams.

Slieve Aughty, Co. Galway

And I myself met once with a young man in the Burren Hills who remembered an old poet who made his poems in Irish and had met when he was young, the young man said, one who called herself Maeve, and said she was a queen 'among them', and asked him if he would have money or pleasure. He said he would have pleasure, and she gave him her love for a time, and then went from him, and ever after he was very mournful. The young man had often heard him sing the poem of lamentation that he made, but could only remember that it was 'very mournful', and that he called her 'beauty of all beauties'.

from *The Celtic Twilight*

The stark landscape of the Burren, Co. Clare

On the grey rock of Cashel the mind's eye
Has called up the cold spirits that are born
When the old moon is vanished from the sky
And the new still hides her horn.

Under blank eyes and fingers never still
The particular is pounded till it is man.
When had I my own will?
O not since life began.

Constrained, arraigned, baffled, bent and unbent
By these wire-jointed jaws and limbs of wood,
Themselves obedient,
Knowing not evil and good;

Obedient to some hidden magical breath.
They do not even feel, so abstract are they,
So dead beyond our death,
Triumph that we obey.

from *The Double Vision of Michael Robartes*

It was at Tulira I decided to evoke the lunar power, which was, I believed, the chief source of my inspiration. I evoked for nine evenings with no great result, but on the ninth night as I was going to sleep I saw first a centaur and then a marvellous naked woman shooting an arrow at a star.

from *Memoirs*

Tulira Castle, Co. Galway, home of Edward Martyn, one of the founders of the Abbey Theatre with Yeats and Lady Gregory

The situation in the centre of the lake . . . is romantic, and at one end, and perhaps at the other too, there is a stone platform where meditative persons might pace to and fro. I planned a mystical Order which should buy or hire the castle, and keep it as a place where its members could retire for a while for contemplation . . . and for ten years to come my most impassioned thought was a vain attempt to find philosophy and to create ritual for that Order.

from *The Trembling of the Veil*

Castle Island, Lough Key, Co. Roscommon

120

Gay bells or sad, they bring you memories
Of half-forgotten innocent old places:
We and our bitterness have left no traces
On Munster grass and Connemara skies.

from The Dedication to a Book of Stories
selected from The Irish Novelists

I came on a great house in the middle of the night,
Its open lighted doorway and its windows all alight,
And all my friends were there and made me welcome too;
But I woke in an old ruin that the winds howled through;
And when I pay attention I must out and walk
Among the dogs and horses that understand my talk.

O what of that, O what of that,
What is there left to say?

from The Curse of Cromwell

Previous page: The hills of Connemara
Right: The ruin of Tyrone House, Co. Galway,
burnt down during the 1920 troubles

124

'Although I'd lie lapped up in linen
A deal I'd sweat and little earn
If I should live as live the neighbours,'
Cried the beggar, Billy Byrne;
'Stretch bones till the daylight come
On great-grandfather's battered tomb.'

Upon a grey old battered tombstone
In Glendalough beside the stream,
Where the O'Byrnes and Byrnes are buried,
He stretched his bones and fell in a dream
Of sun and moon that a good hour
Bellowed and pranced in the round tower;

Of golden king and silver lady,
Bellowing up and bellowing round,
Till toes mastered a sweet measure,
Mouth mastered a sweet sound,
Prancing round and prancing up
Until they pranced upon the top.

from *Under the Round Tower*

The Round Tower, part of the 6th-century monastic
settlement, Glendalough, Co. Wicklow

The hill of Teamhair, or Tara, as it is now called, with its green mounds and its partly wooded sides, and its more gradual slope set among fat grazing lands, with great tress in the hedge-rows, had brought before one imaginations, not of heroes who were in their youth for hundreds of years, or of women who came to them in the likeness of hunted fawns, but of kings that lived brief and politic lives, and of the five white roads that carried their armies to the lesser kingdoms of Ireland, or brought to the great fair that had given Teamhair its sovereignty, all that sought justice or pleasure or had goods to barter.

from *Gods and Fighting Men*

Statue of St Patrick, the Hill of Tara, Co. Meath, ancient seat of the Kings of Ireland

And I rode by the plains of the sea's edge, where all is barren and grey,
Grey sand on the green of the grasses and over the dripping trees,
Dripping and doubling landward, as though they would hasten away,
Like an army of old men longing for rest from the moan of the seas.

And the winds made the sands on the sea's edge turning and turning go,
As my mind made the names of the Fenians. Far from the hazel and oak,
I rode away on the surges, where, high as the saddle-bow,
Fled foam underneath me, and round me, a wandering and milky smoke.

from *The Wanderings of Oisin*

Seashore in County Kerry

Who Goes with Fergus?

Who will go drive with Fergus now,
And pierce the deep wood's woven shade,
And dance upon the level shore?
Young man, lift up your russet brow,
And lift your tender eyelids, maid,
And brood on hopes and fear no more.

And no more turn aside and brood
Upon love's bitter mystery;
For Fergus rules the brazen cars,
And rules the shadows of the wood,
And the white breast of the dim sea
And all dishevelled wandering stars.

The Cliffs of Moher, Co. Clare

THE NINETEENTH CENTURY
AND AFTER

Though the great song return no more
There's keen delight in what we have:
The rattle of pebbles on the shore
Under the receding wave.

A lone curragh rests on the pebbled Connemara shore

Some day we shall get up before the dawn
And find our ancient hounds before the door,
And wide awake know that the hunt is on;
Stumbling upon the blood-dark track once more,
Then stumbling to the kill beside the shore;
Then cleaning out and bandaging of wounds,
And chants of victory amid the encircling hounds.

from *Hound Voice*

Hunting in County Kilkenny

The wind blows out of the gates of the day,
The wind blows over the lonely of heart,
And the lonely of heart is withered away.
While the faeries dance in a place apart,
Shaking their milk-white feet in a ring,
Tossing their milk-white arms in the air;
For they hear the wind laugh and murmur and sing
Of a land where even the old are fair,
And even the wise are merry of tongue;
But I heard a reed of Coolaney say,
'When the wind has laughed and murmured and sung
The lonely of heart is withered away!'

from *The Land of Heart's Desire*

'Coolaney Lake' (Lough Gill)

DUBLIN

I had very little money and one day the toll-taker at the metal bridge over the Liffey and a gossip of his laughed when I refused the halfpenny and said, 'No, I will go round by O'Connell Bridge.'

from *Reveries over Childhood and Youth*

The Metal Bridge (or Halfpenny Bridge) on the river Liffey

Go, unquiet wanderer,
And gather the Glasnevin coverlet
About your head till the dust stops your ear,
The time for you to taste of that salt breath
And listen at the corners has not come;
You had enough of sorrow before death –
Away, away! You are safer in the tomb.

from *To a Shade*

Parnell's statue, O'Connell Street

At other times, I would sleep among the rhododendrons and rocks in the wilder part of the grounds of Howth Castle. After a while my father said I must stay indoors half the night, meaning that I should get some sleep in my bed; but I, knowing that I would be too sleepy and comfortable to get up again used to sit over the kitchen fire till half the night was gone.

from *Reveries over Childhood and Youth*

My London school-fellow, the athlete, spent a summer with us, but the friendship of boyhood, founded upon action and adventure, was drawing to an end . . . One morning I proposed a journey to Lambay Island, and was contemptuous because he said we should miss our mid-day meal. We hoisted a sail on our small boat and ran quickly over the nine miles and saw on the shore a tame sea-gull, while a couple of boys, the sons of a coastguard, ran into the water in their clothes to pull us to land, as we had read of savage people doing. We spent an hour upon the sunny shore and I said, 'I would like to live here always, and perhaps some day I will.' I was always discovering places where I would like to spend my whole life.

from *Reveries over Childhood and Youth*

Lambay Island, Co. Dublin 147

SWIFT'S EPITAPH

Swift has sailed into his rest;
Savage indignation there
Cannot lacerate his breast.
Imitate him if you dare,
World-besotted traveller; he
Served human liberty.

148

Swift's monument, St Patrick's Cathedral

I write it out in a verse –
MacDonagh and MacBride
And Connolly and Pearse
Now and in time to be,
Wherever green is worn,
Are changed, changed utterly:
A terrible beauty is born.

from *Easter 1916*

Kilmainham Jail, scene of the fifteen
executions after the 1916 rising

I was among Unionists, and some young
landlord, a dull, not unkindly man, told
how he was peeping through a hotel window at a public meeting that had been
called to support his tenants against him.
Somebody had shouted from the audience,
'Shoot him,' and a beautiful girl upon the
platform, whom he believed to be Maud
Gonne, had clapped her hands. My uncle,
George Pollexfen, with obvious reluctance,
not wishing to speak against any friend of
mine, hinted that he knew of his own
knowledge something very bad about her. 'I
once saw her,' and here he stopped to
explain what had brought him to Dublin,
'in the hall of the Gresham Hotel speaking
to Mr William Redmond. What will not
women do for notoriety?' He considered all
Nationalist members of parliament as
socially impossible.

from *Memoirs*

Gresham Hotel, O'Connell Street, which was
destroyed in the Civil War of 1922, rebuilt and
reopened in 1927

The one house where nobody thought or talked politics was a house in Ely Place, where a number of young men lived together, and, for want of a better name, were called Theosophists. Beside the resident members, other members dropped in and out during the day, and the reading-room was a place of much discussion about philosophy and about the arts. The house had been taken in the name of the engineer to the Board of Works, a black-bearded young man, with a passion for Manichean philosophy, and all accepted him as host; and sometimes the conversation, especially when I was there, became too ghostly for the nerves of his young and delicate wife, and he would be made angry. I remember young men struggling, with inexact terminology and insufficient learning, for some new religious conception, on which they could base their lives; and some few strange or able men.

from *The Trembling of the Veil*

8, Ely Place, where Yeats, George Russell and Maud Gonne among others, attended meetings of the Dublin Theosophical Society

153

What need you, being come to sense,
But fumble in a greasy till
And add the halfpence to the pence
And prayer to shivering prayer, until
You have dried the marrow from the bone?
For men were born to pray and save:
Romantic Ireland's dead and gone,
It's with O'Leary in the grave . . ..

from *September 1913*

Come gather round me, players all:
Come praise Nineteen-Sixteen,
Those from the pit and gallery
Or from the painted scene
That fought in the Post Office
Or round the City Hall,
Praise every man that came again,
Praise every man that fell.

From mountain to mountain ride the fierce horsemen.

from *Three Songs to the One Burden*

The Post Office, scene of the doomed insurrection of 1916

Under bare Ben Bulben's head
In Drumcliff churchyard Yeats is laid . . . .

Cast a cold eye
On life, on death.
Horseman, pass by!

from *Under Ben Bulben*

Yeats died in the south of France in 1939 but, as he had wished, his remains were brought back to Drumcliff churchyard, Sligo

INDEX

At Galway Races   111

Blood and the Moon   88, 95

Celtic Twilight, The   26, 32, 41, 55, 58, 87, 114
Coole Park, 1929   34-5, 85
Curse of Cromwell, The   124

Dedication to a book of stories selected from the
   Irish novelists   124
Dialogue of Self and Soul, A   93
Double Vision of Michael Robartes, The   116
Down by the Salley Gardens   75
Dreaming of the Bones, The   104

Easter 1916   149

Fiddler of Dooney, The   49

'Gods and Fighting' Men   129

Hosting of the Sidhe, The   62
Hound Voice   137

I am of Ireland   98

In Memory of Eva Gore-Booth and Con
   Markiewicz   65
In Memory of Major Robert Gregory   97, 101
In the Seven Woods   79

Lake Isle of Innisfree, The   34
Land of Heart's Desire, The   138

Man and the Echo, The   37
Man who Dreamed of Faeryland, The   69
Meditations in Time of Civil War   94
Meditation of the Old Fisherman, The   25
Memoirs   65, 70, 119, 150

Nineteenth Century and After, The   135

Old Men Admiring Themselves in the Water,
   The   45
Only Jealousy of Emer, The   50

Pilgrim, The   108
Prayer on Going into My House, A   90
Preface to J.M. Synge's 'The Well of the
   Saints'   107

Red Hanrahan's Song about Ireland   42
Reveries over Childhood and Youth   20, 23, 28, 46, 66
   73, 140, 144, 147

Secret Rose, The   31
September 1913   155
Stolen Child, The   52, 56
Swift's Epitaph   148

Three Songs to the One Burden   156
To a Child Dancing in the Wind   61
To a Shade   143
Towards Break of Day   38
Trembling of the Veil, The   76, 120, 152

Under Ben Bulben   159
Under the Round Tower   127
Upon a House shaken by the Land
   Agitation   80

Wanderings of Oisin, The   130
Who Goes with Fergus?   132
Wild Swans of Coole, The   82
Withering of the Boughs, The   112